Slithering SNAKES

Sarah Creese

make
believe
ideas

Slithering snakes have scaly skin.
They can climb up trees and even swim!
With a flickering tongue they taste the air.
Now let's explore them – if you dare!

Copyright © 2010 make believe ideas ltd.
27 Castle Street, Berkhamsted, Hertfordshire, HP4 2DW.

Slithering Snakes

Reading together

This book is an ideal first reader for your child, combining simple words and sentences with stunning colour photography of real-life snakes. Here are some of the many ways you can help your child take those first steps in reading.

Encourage your child to:

- Look at and explore the detail in the pictures.
- Sound out the letters in each word.
- Read and repeat each short sentence.

Look at the pictures

Make the most of each page by talking about the pictures and spotting key words. Here are some questions you can use to discuss each page as you go along:

- Why do you like this snake?
- What would it feel like to touch?
- What colour is it?
- Does it look friendly or scary?

Look at rhymes

Some of the sentences in this book are simple rhymes. Encourage your child to recognise rhyming words. Try asking the following questions:

- What does this word say?
- Can you find a word that rhymes with it?

- Look at the ending of two words that rhyme. Are they spelled the same? For example, "hot" and "spot", and "trees" and "seas".

Test understanding

It is one thing to understand the meaning of individual words, but you need to check that your child understands the facts in the text.

- Play "spot the obvious mistake". Read the text as your child looks at the words with you, but make an obvious mistake to see if he or she catches it. Ask your child to correct you and provide the right word.
- After reading the facts, shut the book and make up questions to ask your child.
- Ask your child whether a fact is true or false.
- Provide your child with three answers to a question and ask him or her to pick the correct one.

Quiz pages

At the end of the book there is a simple quiz. Ask the questions and see if your child can remember the right answers from the text. If not, encourage him or her to look up the answers.

Snakes

Snakes can live in many different places around the world, from deserts to the sea.

Grass Snake

I'm a slithering snake
with no arms or legs.
I can be long or short
and I can lay eggs.

Hatching Green Tree Python

Green Tree Python

To warm up,
I lie somewhere hot.
To cool down again,
I find a shady spot.

Garter Snake

My bendy body
is covered with scales.
Watch out for
my rattling tail!

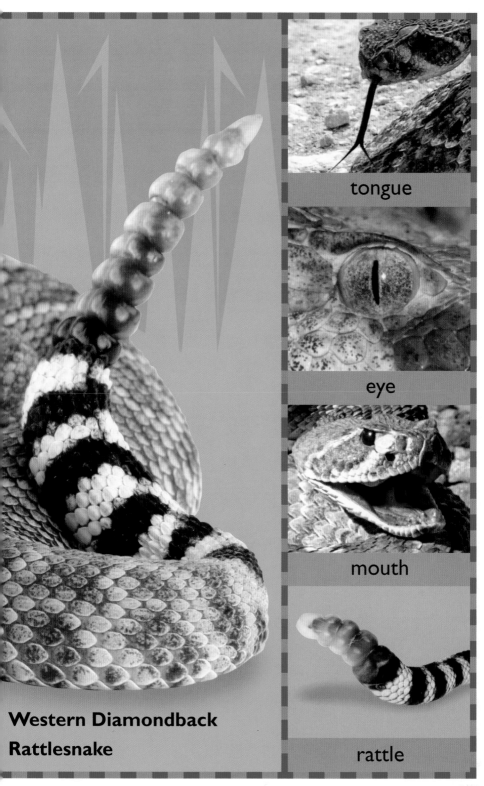

**Western Diamondback
Rattlesnake**

tongue

eye

mouth

rattle

13

Northern Watersnake

I live on land,
in deserts and trees.
I can swim underwater
and live in the seas!

I shed my skin.
It's quite a show!
I do this so that
I can grow.

old skin

new skin

Dione Ratsnake

Boa Constrictor

I use my tongue
to taste the air.
It helps me smell
things everywhere!

Sipo

Cape Cobra

Pinesnake

**Red-Sided
Gartersnake**

19

Egg-Eating Snake

I'm an egg-eating snake.
Can you tell?
I swallow eggs whole,
then spit out the shell!

Egg is swallowed whole

Egg bulges in snake's bo

Egg breaks

Snake spits out the shell

21

Milksnake

I can kill my prey
by squeezing tight
in the day or in the night.

I can stretch my mouth
to eat a whole deer!
When I'm feeling hungry,
it's best to keep clear.

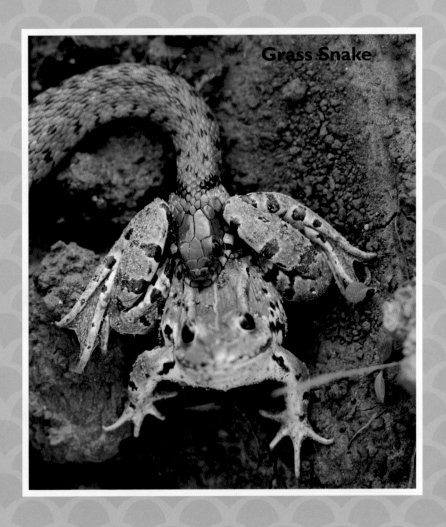

Grass Snake

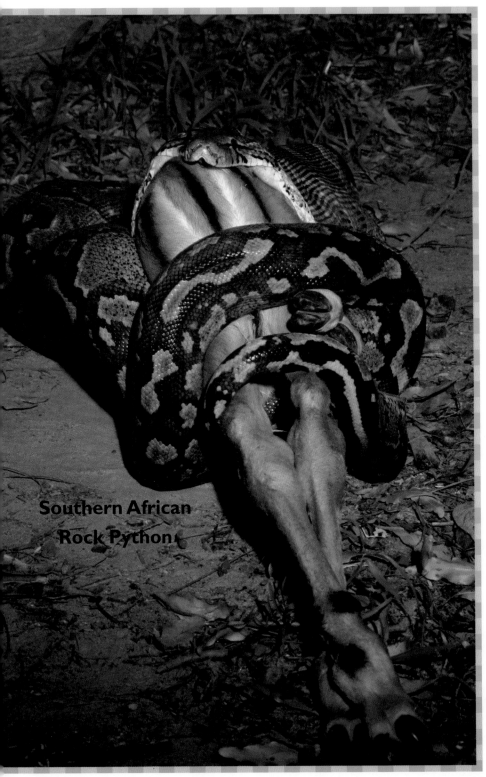

Southern African
Rock Python

My colourful body
is red and black;
it warns my enemies
not to attack!

Key words

Here are some key words used in context.
Make simple sentences for the other words
in the border.

I **am** a snake.

My body **is** red
and black.

I **can** lay eggs.

I use my tongue
to taste the air.

I **have** scaly skin.

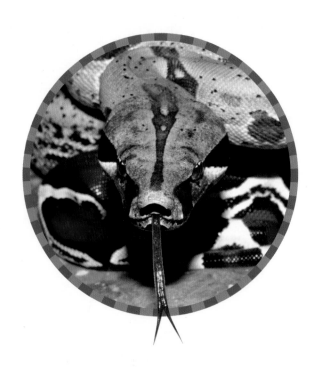